TRANSFORMED
from My Image to His Image

DR. VALERIE KITCHENS

WESTBOW
PRESS®
A DIVISION OF THOMAS NELSON
& ZONDERVAN

This book is a work of non-fiction. Unless otherwise noted, the author and the publisher make no explicit guarantees as to the accuracy of the information contained in this book and in some cases, names of people and places have been altered to protect their privacy.

Scripture taken from the King James Version of the Bible.

"Scripture taken from the NEW AMERICAN STANDARD BIBLE®, Copyright © 1960,1962,1963,1968,1971,1972,1973,1975,1977,199 5 by The Lockman Foundation. Used by permission."

Scripture quotations marked (NLT) are taken from the Holy Bible, New Living Translation, copyright © 1996, 2004, 2007 by Tyndale House Foundation. Used by permission of Tyndale House Publishers, Inc., Carol Stream, Illinois 60188. All rights reserved.

WestBow Press books may be ordered through booksellers or by contacting:

WestBow Press
A Division of Thomas Nelson & Zondervan
1663 Liberty Drive
Bloomington, IN 47403
www.westbowpress.com
1 (866) 928-1240

Because of the dynamic nature of the Internet, any web addresses or links contained in this book may have changed since publication and may no longer be valid. The views expressed in this work are solely those of the author and do not necessarily reflect the views of the publisher, and the publisher hereby disclaims any responsibility for them.

Any people depicted in stock imagery provided by Getty Images are models, and such images are being used for illustrative purposes only. Certain stock imagery © Getty Images.

ISBN: 978-1-9736-4463-7 (sc)
ISBN: 978-1-9736-4464-4 (e)

Library of Congress Control Number: 2018913207

Print information available on the last page.

WestBow Press rev. date: 11/06/2018

About the Author

Dr. Valerie Kitchens is an ordained minister and founder of Earth Changers International Ministries in Fort Worth, Texas. Dr. Kitchens has traveled extensively nationally and internationally preaching and teaching the holy scriptures and making disciples. She is also an educator who values deep, rich understanding of truth and is passionate about dispelling myths and errors while guiding others to truth.

Her experience in ministry taught her that many teachers, especially Americans, limit the Christian learners' ability to understand the holy scriptures by restricting their studies to "American interruption" verses digging deep and unlocking the hidden treasures of the correct content of the scriptures through the Jewish setting or culture. Dr. Kitchens's passion for truth caused her to seek understanding of God's Word through the divine revelation of the Holy Spirit and the historical accounts and setting of the Jewish culture; she created a common ground for American interpretation in a very simple way for easy reading and without losing the intended meaning.

Dr. Kitchens holds a doctorate in education in organizational leadership, a master's in religious education, a master's in discipleship ministries, and a bachelor of science degree in health and sports science.

Special Dedication

To my heavenly Father, who gave me the courage to write and the insight for what to say. Without Him, none of this would have been possible.

To my beloved baby girl, Rachel Maria Kitchens, who truly understands the meaning of being transformed when she departed this world on March 9, 2012, at age eighteen.

When you were born, you cried only three seconds before observing the new world you were entering. I knew then that there was something special about you. You possessed a great amount of courage and strength that was a comfort to all. Love you forever, Sweetie Peaty, and miss you dearly.

To my son, Micah Kitchens—you have been a rock in my life. Your kind and gentle spirit has always touched my heart. One thing I love about you is your competitive nature and consistent ways. You are truly Da Man. I love you with all my heart, and it is a pleasure watching you mature into a fine young man.

Last, I dedicated this book to my three best friends and spiritual sisters: Dr. Arlene Horne, Cheryl Minick, and LaTania Moore. People say it is impossible for women to be close friends without jealousy and strife, but you all have proven that wrong. You have believed in me and the vision God poured into me, and for that, I am forever grateful for our eternal friendship.

Abstract

New believers can find starting a new spiritual walk overwhelming at the start. They may ask themselves where to begin, what to read, and how to get involved. They may look to others who have been on that path for a long time to determine how they are embracing their Christianity.

Some believers may attend only Sunday worship service while others may attend only midweek services such as small groups or Bible study. More-engaged believers might attend all the services and be involved in choir and youth ministry. Christians can do great things in the ministries they engage in, but is that what they need to transform the lives of new converts? God wants His children to live a certain way and learn who He is, what to expect of Him, and what He expects of them. This lifestyle is what I call a truly transformed life.

Transformed is a journey I want to take with serious believers who want more than just a Sunday experience. *Transformed* is looking for people who want to walk in the victorious life and freedom the Spirit of the Lord offers us. *Transformed* is looking for believers who want to overcome this world, live empowered lives, and walk in the image of God, their Father. *Transformed* is here to help you understand what it means to transition from one state to another, leaving what you know and desire behind for the lifestyle and desires God has chosen for you. It's a matter of walking out of your comfort zone into the transformed life awaiting you. Submitted vessels are willing to forgo their will and accept the chosen lifestyle and will designed by another—God the Father—and transform from their image to His image.

Contents

Introduction

Can two walk together, except they be agreed.
—Amos 3:3

In January 2013, I was invited to Kentucky to minister at a women's conference, and during my preparation in seeking God for the right message, He gave me this scripture: "Can two walk together, except they be agreed" (Amos 3:3). Many people often misquote this scripture by stopping short at "can two walk together." As I wrote this scripture down, I took a closer look at its meaning. In the first part of the scripture, it pose the question "Can two walk together?" That seems easy to answer, right? Nevertheless, it is far from that. Before explaining the first part, let us consider the rest of the passage: "except they be agreed."

The second part provides the necessary information for understanding the first part. For two to walk together in agreement, they must decide all that is to happen before they can come to an agreement. For example, people make new year's resolutions to get in shape, save money, or other declarations. That, however, is just the idea. The second part of the plan is the action, and the final part is the agreement.

Someone might want to lose thirty pounds; that's the idea. The action is how that will happen. Here is an example of an action plan.

1. Examine the current diet to adjust calorie intake
2. Exercise.
3. Get proper rest.
4. Follow through with the plan.

The above is an action plan that was discussed, planned, and considered. If both parts are accepted—the idea to lose weight and the action taken to achieve that—the two can walk together in agreement to achieve a new lifestyle. This is how the working of the Father and Holy Spirit operates together. The Holy Spirit is the action or power working the ideas of God. In Genesis 1 is an example of this concept: "God said, let there be light" was the idea, and "and there was light" was the action; a perfect model of two working together in agreement.

If the Holy Spirit chose to operate on His own will, what would He create? The Holy Spirit may have the power and ability to do that, but where is the idea of the Father? If the idea wasn't given by the Father, the Holy Spirit would be acting on His own and not be in agreement with the Father. The unsubmitted vessel is like that. But what is the idea of God, and how does it fit in the scheme of things?

I wrote this book to explore the lives of unregenerate hearts, new believers, and those seeking courage to let go of this world, not to conform to it but transform from it to become to the image God desires.

Each chapter examines each concept of the transformation process and establishes a simple and comprehensive plan to work in partnership with the Holy Spirit to transform.

The first chapter explains the concept of transform. Chapter 2 defines the author's meaning of the phrase *my image* and provides a snapshot of my life before my transformation. Chapter 3 deals with the image the Father sees. In Chapters 4 through 6, I detail the idea, the action, and the agreement. The last chapter is a study guide you can use as a model to begin the transformation process.

CHAPTER 1
My Image

For as he thinketh in his heart, so is he: Eat and drink,
saith he to thee; but his heart is not with thee.
—Proverbs 23:7

My image. Hmmm. What does that mean? Let's consider these two words. The most important word to examine first is *my*. According to Dictionary.com, *my* means "of, belonging to, or associated with the speaker or writer (me): my own ideas." The other word is *image*. According to Dictionary.com, an *image* is a mental representation, an idea, or a conception. So my image is my mental representation of myself. Here is the raw deal: no matter what others may say about me, it's what I see of myself that's important.

In the next few pages, I expose my life to allow you to identify with my sufferings and understand that no matter what happens in the lowest, darkest places of your life, the Father's love is able to forgive all and help them transform into His image.

My Mental Representation of Myself

As far back as I can remember, I was inquisitive, creative, and athletic. Born November 24, 1968, at an air force base in Ohio the last of seven children, of a family living on an air force base in the Midwest, my memories started in Michigan. One of the most memorable times in my life was when I was around four and living in that state. My mother loved being around water; it didn't matter if it was an ocean, beach, lake, or stream—wherever we lived, my mom always found water—which meant swimming for me.

During one outing to a lake, I felt that the water was calling me to explore its depths. Not the creatures under the water—just the depth. My curiosity drove me to find out how far the bottom was from the surface, and it took all the strength I had to keep my life jacket on. I knew it was supposed to keep me afloat, but it was keeping me from reaching the bottom of the lake.

I also remember that around the same time and place, I loved climbing trees. Just outside our back door was a large tree I loved to climb. The problem was that while I loved climbing up, I was afraid of the descent. So each time I climbed the tree, my mother had to come out to guide me down.

A third memory dealt with airplanes. Somehow, I got the idea that I knew how to build airplanes, and I tried hard to construct one. One day while sitting by a pile of lumber, I put together what my mind conceived as a flyable plane; all I needed was a place high enough to launch it, and I knew if I launch the plane, from the roof of my house, I would soar into the clouds. My mother's intervention saved my life.

We moved back to the state of my birth, and my mom allowed me to participate in karate, ballet, gymnastics, and soccer. I participated for six months in each for free; after that, my parents were required to pay. I later found out that they had been unable to pay, and that's why I had to stop participating in those activities.

I attended a school with a state-of-the-art gym; because I had some experience in gymnastics, I couldn't wait to show off my talent. Besides that, I dreamed of running in the Olympics; I was very fast. One day, the PE teacher and coach asked me to run against some girls. The two instructors then put me with a group of boys to run against, and then the coach started selecting some faster and older boys for me to run against. I noticed the coach was timing me, and he asked me to run on a youth track team. I was sad to tell him I was about to move even though I had been at the school for only about three weeks. The coach begged me not to move, but I told him he would have to address my family about that. I knew in my heart I had what it took to be an Olympic athlete, and the look in my coach's eye confirmed that.

Later on, my family moved to Kentucky, where my athletic side really bloomed. I was in the fourth or fifth grade (around the late seventies to early eighties). I did not like sitting around in a slow town and feeling I was idling; instead, I always looked for something to do. Once, I walked by my elementary school and saw people participating in a punt, pass, and kick competition, so I signed up. Never mind I was the only girl there and had never picked up a football; I knew in my heart that I was better.

A few weeks later, I observed people signing up for a 10k race. Though I had no concept of the distance and didn't have any time to prepare for it—yes, you guessed it—I signed up and ran.

During a gym class, the coach introduced me to basketball—and I was a natural at it. My first tryout landed me on the higher-level basketball team as a first-year player. And last but not least, the first time ever I played softball, I was voted MVP for the whole league. Amazing, right? The coach's son called me the king of home runs because every time I got up to bat, I hit one.

After returning to my birth state in the eighties, I continued rising in athletics. My ability couldn't be matched. Throughout high school, I was a strong swimmer, a developed diver, and a highly competitive basketball player, sprinter, and softball player.

My athletic career did not stop there. In the late eighties, I joined the military, and all throughout my career there, I continued in sports as I continue to do today. Now, I'm coaching so I can pass on my knowledge and skills.

If I would stop here, my life might seem pretty dynamic and promising for a very strong athletic future. But there is another side of my life that followed me—it was full of pain, shame, and disappointment that broke me from relying on and trusting people and their promises.

When I was about four, I once stood with my older sibling next to the bed my mom was sitting on. She was at the middle of the mattress but sitting at the edge, slumped over with her hands to her face and crying harder than I had ever seen anyone do. All I can remember was asking God to take the pain from my mom, to allow me to carry the pain for her. Somehow, I felt strong enough to do so. For years, I carried those memories in my heart but did not remember enough of the details to release the pain.

However, in the late nineties, I was with my sibling in a room and I asked about that situation. My sibling couldn't believe I remembered the incident because I had been so young—three, my sibling said. As soon as my sibling began describing the situation, I felt something grip my heart; the pain was removed, and the memory no longer plagued me.

The clearer picture of the story was that my mom was obviously upset because of the marital situation and asked me if I wanted to go see God—and I said yes. Our family was very involved with church, and I had a great love for the Lord even at that age. When I said yes, I was given something to take along with my sibling—but my sibling knew something wasn't quite right and took what had been placed in my hand away from all of us. My sibling then laid my mom down and pulled the covers up to let them cry themselves to sleep as my sibling took me out of the room. I didn't realize until later what was being attempted.

The next challenge in my life was the constant moving, but as long as my parents were together, I felt stable. However, before my teen years, all that changed. Before my parents were together, my mom had been married for years to a military man. My mom's parents had passed away when she was young. Though my mother had her grandmother and older siblings, she lived with another family after her parents passed away, and I don't know why. Because her conditions were difficult, my mom got married to a military man, had children, and traveled the world. Many hardships came about, and that marriage dissolved. Then my parents came together and had more children.

In time, my parents split up and my world got worse. Because my mom did not have the best education, she had difficulty finding jobs, and that meant we moved frequently. In my youth, I never lived anywhere longer than three years. Once, I counted the schools I attended—thirty-six elementary schools, one middle school, and three high schools in many states. Any person can guess at this point that I was underdeveloped academically and socially. But even in the most broken part of my life, I became determined to obtain two master's degrees (in physical therapy and in sports medicine) and a doctorate in psychology.

Growing up, I was an oddly quiet person. I wasn't shy; I just would not talk to anyone. I assumed the reason was due to my constant moving, and I lost many friends because I wouldn't talk.

On a positive note, in the fifth grade, I was looking for paper to sketch on when I entered a closet that contained many books, including encyclopedias. I looked through them and uncovered a world I had never known existed. At that time, I promised myself that I would have things in every room of my house that came from all over the world.

In the '70s, my parents worked at General Electric in a major city and owned lots of land. My dad built the house my mom had designed. We had a side-by-side refrigerator with an icemaker, a microwave, a gas stove with a built-in grill, and bar stools at the breakfast counter. My sibling and I had our own beds with huge smiling faces painted on the wall like headboards. Sliding glass doors led to the backyard, and a U-shaped driveway led to and from the house. I did not know how well off we were until my parents went their separate ways and our finances became rocky. I had to watch how my mom obtained food and clothes for us. The real pain was seeing her have to turn to family members for help. I hated every trip to that place because I saw the pain and embarrassment my mom had to endure due to her family's humiliating lectures. Seeing that look on my mom's face was horrible. Then after all that anguish, we ended up being fed and clothed anyway. For the life of me, I couldn't understand why we were put through all that only to be helped in the end. The clothes I had to wear were hand-me-downs from male cousins that did not fit properly, and the money my mother received went to the upkeep of our car and house. I can't remember a time I received new clothes or even hair ribbons.

The last part of my life was the hardest and was a combination of many things. First, I watched new relationships in my mother's life after my dad had left. I knew that if my mother were without her children, maybe one of her relationships would have worked out. It was plain to see that the men in my mom's life wanted her, not us, and I felt unwanted.

She often left us with people she knew but were strangers to me, and that made me scared and insecure. One time, I was with a babysitter, and a man who came along with the babysitter molested me. I found out later he was a minister. Shortly after that, another babysitter molested me; both incidents happened in the same year while I was in grade school. Later, I found out that the molesters were of the same family. Crazy, right?

Having been violated by both led me to live a very lonely, neutral life; I did not want to be with anybody. I was bullied going to school every day by twin sisters who sought the help of a boy who had flunked two years in a row because the sisters wouldn't fight me and my sibling but the boy would. The twin sisters were jealous of me because of my light-skinned complexion, dark-brown and naturally wavy hair, and my ability to answer questions in class. I could not understand why they were jealous; I was just trying to survive.

The next dramatic thing that really pushed me to live a narrow life was watching a major, life-altering change in my sibling's life at an early age. The situation was not positive, and because it was so unusual, it changed our family's dynamics. When our community became aware of the situation, they turned against us rather than helping us. We became the talk of the town, and people made fun of me because they could not get to my sibling. That incident built up lots anger in me because all the plans and dreams we promised each other were gone. We were the Williams sisters of the time destroyed through choices, and that put a big wedge in our relationship. I wanted nothing to do with the relationship.

In addition to that, Alex Haley's *Roots* came out; so on top of being plagued by negative comments, I was now being called the *N* word by some of the school children; I lived in a predominately white area. Many black people considered me high yellow or light skinned, and neither blacks nor whites like me because I wasn't one of them. On top of all that, my formerly tight relationship with my family was strained. To make matters worse, I lived under the shadow of others' beauty. I couldn't catch any boys' eyes after they saw my siblings. I had no hope. Rejected by blacks and whites, molested, with a nonsupportive family and broken sibling relationships—what was I to do? Where was I to turn?

In time, my pain led me to strong negative behavior, which was putting me in a dangerous place though I was still holding onto athletics. I started hanging with the wrong people and making the worst choices of my life, which opened the door to a rape and a beating. That's when I knew I needed to get out. Amazing, right? These were only highlights of my life, and believe it or not, all that had happened before I was eighteen.

I spent twenty two years after high school in the military, but I carried scars from my past; that was evident in the photo they took of me in basic training. In 1990, I deployed to Saudi Arabia during Desert Shield/Storm, where I sustained an injury to my right ankle. The injury threatened my military career and life as an athlete. The surgery I needed was a triple arthrodesis, which involved fusing bones in my foot. The orthopedic surgeon informed me that if had the surgery, I would not be able to run again, but if I didn't have the surgery, I would be medically boarded and put out of the military. Hard choice, right?

Before I decided about the surgery, I went home to visit my mom since I had just come home from the war. While at home, I hung out with an old friend, and we were drinking and more. We decided late that evening to visit some military friends of mine in a southern state. About forty-five minutes into the trip, my body shut down. I was talking and asleep at the same time, and I rolled my car three times when I was doing seventy-five. We fortunately had our seat belts on. I would have been responsible for her death as she later told me her head had hit the ground. I had hit my head on the windshield, but I walked away with no scratches.

I hit rock bottom in my life, and after returning to my duty station broken, I still had to make a major decision—I had the surgery. I was twenty-one in 1991, just before my transformation begun.

What I See

If I asked you what you thought of my life, would you see my promising future that was initially shining through? Looking at both sides of my life, how could I create an accurate mental representation of myself or a compiled sketched of my image? I stepped back to consider that question, and this is what I saw: a five-five, 130-pound, light-skinned, slender, muscular, athletic girl with dark-brown, wavy hair, a free-spirited and loving person who wanted only the best for others, and a giving and very trusting person who loved adventure. I saw a highly gifted athlete who had no limits to what she could do. I saw someone who loved helping others make their dreams come true. I saw someone who gave her last to people in need without regard for her own needs.

On the other hand, I saw a young girl living in isolation, pain, and anger due to being poor and rejected. The more I wanted love, the more pain I received. Where was the joy? Where was the peace? Where were the promises all the people around me had made to me? I saw a person who wanted to be recognized for her contributions and added value to the team; someone who wanted to feel valued and considered an asset. I saw someone who wanted to know that what she did mattered to others.

On one plate, I had been served brokenness, rejection, and emptiness; on another plate, I had received an athletic gift strong enough to stabilize the madness and imbalances in my life. That was me in a nutshell before marriage and children, but that's another hardship to tell.

CHAPTER 2
The Concept of Transformation

I beseech you therefore, brethren, by the mercies of God, that ye
present your bodies a living sacrifice, holy, acceptable unto God,
which is your reasonable service. And be not conformed to this world:
but be ye transformed by the renewing of your mind, that ye may
prove what is that good, and acceptable, and perfect, will of God.
—Romans 12:1–2

When I was a child, every Saturday morning, I woke up early, headed to the kitchen for some Fruity Pebbles cereal that I put in the largest bowl along with three teaspoons of sugar and enough milk to take up the rest of the room. I carefully walked with it to the living room trying not to spill any, and that process felt like eternity.

In the living room, I sat my bowl of cereal on the coffee table and went to my bedroom for a blanket and pillow that I would put on a heat register to warm them up. I'd lie propped up on my pillow covered in my blanket to eat my cereal and watch cartoons including *The Really Rottens*, *The Jetsons*, and *Transformers*. *The Jetsons* and *Transformers* captivated me with their futuristic lifestyles and advanced technology, but *Transformers* dealt with issues of good and evil. The good side always fought for the rights and freedom of others, and at the end of each episode, life lessons or moral issues were explained to show that the Decepticons' ways were in error and that if they changed their hearts, that would make the world a better place. Plus, I found it interesting how they hid their advanced technology in everyday items such as cars and trucks but when needed, the five or so cars and trucks transformed from cars and trucks into a unified body, a robot with amazing strength to face the enemy. Their former individual identities merged into a single robot. As their iconic logo says, Transformers were "More Than Meets the Eye."

Who would have thought a cartoon those many years ago would spearhead a spiritual concept? How does all this tie together to explain the concept of being transformed? Easy. The major wow factor for Transformers was their ability to move between two states. To remain undercover, the highly advanced technological forms hid their identities in objects such as cars and trucks and transformed when trouble arose. At the command, "Autobots assemble!" each vehicle rose into the air and became individual segments of the robot. The reverse would happen when danger was conquered, and they would drive in a convoy to their next assignment.

We will not be transitioned from cars to robotic figures, but we are asked to transform. Romans 12:2 states, "And be not conformed to this world: but be ye **transformed** by the renewing of your mind that ye may prove what is that good, and acceptable, and perfect, will of God." Dictionary.com defines the word *transform* as to change one thing into another; to change from one form, appearance, structure, or type to another.

Rereading the last part of the scripture gives us insight into the final part of the concept of transformation. The Blue Letter Bible identifies *metamorphoo* as a Greek phrase for "be ye transformed." We have to change from one form to another. Another part of the verse indicates that the believer "be not conformed to this world." The Blue Letter Bible also indicates that the Greek word for "conformed" is *syschematizo* meaning to conform one's self, mind, or character to another's pattern. Believers must not let their minds and characters take the form of another pattern, one of this world; they have to change from the form of the world to another, the kingdom of God.

The latter part of the scripture tells the believer to "prove" (Greek *dokimazo*)—to scrutinize something to determine if it is genuine. Four factors will aid in this endeavor: renew your mind, prove what is good, prove what is acceptable, and prove what is the perfect will of God.

Longtime and new believers alike need to understand the depths of this scripture; transformation is a challenging process that requires time and effort. That concept is the point of this book.

CHAPTER 3
The Idea

I will take you back to the Introduction in which we discussed Amos 3:3: "Can two walk together, except they be agreed." We also discussed the importance of an idea, an action plan, and an agreement. In the next two chapters, I will deal with the action plan and the agreement, but in this chapter, I will deal with how it all starts—an idea. The best way to understand this section is by returning to where it all started—Genesis.

Genesis means the origin, the beginning—the idea. One scripture I love reciting is Hebrews 11:10 (NASB): "He was looking for the city which has foundations, whose <u>architect and builder is God</u>."

The idea God had was the creation of the heaven and the earth: "In the beginning God created the heaven and the earth" (Genesis 1:1). In Genesis 1, a good number of verses start with the words "and God said." Before He created anything, He always stated what would occur—the idea—before the action materialized it. Bringing the previous example into focus, the idea here is simple: we are to be transformed from our image to His. God has spoken the idea of what He has created us to be.

Let's develop the idea that we should be transformed. I will mention again my idea of a resolution to lose weight. Say, "I want to lose weight." Did your memory take you back to that perfect size and weight you were in high school or as a young adult? That happens with most people when they think about it. That is what I am trying to get across here; this chapter will conclude with an image or concept of what being transformed should look like.

God has called believers out of the world (spiritually, not physically) into a personal and corporate purity in the midst of sinful cultures.

Biblical separation is usually considered in two areas: personal and ecclesiastical (the church) or in a layperson's terms, spiritually.

Personal separation involves an individual's commitment to a godly standard of behavior, and an ecclesiastical separation involves the decisions of a church concerning its ties to other organizations, based on their theology or practices. To become 100 percent transformed, 100 percent of our personal nature must change and 100 percent of our spiritual being must change.

To examine this a little closer, I will pull apart the personal life from the ecclesiastical (church/spiritual) life. The first consideration as a believer is that our lives belong to God and we are not in control: "I have been crucified with Christ. It is no longer I who live, but Christ who lives in me. And the life I now live in the flesh I live by faith in the Son of God, who loved me and gave himself for me" (Galatians 2:20 ESV). Since my life is not mine, I cannot go wherever I want or do whatever I want; I have to become an obedient child to the one my life now belongs to. "As obedient children, do not be conformed to the passions of your former ignorance, but as he who called you is holy, you also be holy in all your conduct, since it is written, 'You shall be holy, for I am holy'" (1 Peter 1:14–16 ESV).

I must live a life separated from the things I previously participated in. My life must show a difference. I must be aware of my surroundings at all times and the fellowship I keep: "Abstain from every form of evil" (1 Thessalonians 5:22 ESV).

I cannot eat what I want so that I can discern good from evil; I must exercise control: "But Daniel resolved that he would not defile himself with the king's food, or with the wine that he drank. Therefore he asked the chief of the eunuchs to allow him not to defile himself" (Daniel 1:8 ESV). Daniel purposed in his heart that he did not want to sin against God to go with the crowd; he knew God's requirements and standards.

I am warned not to pick up the habits or ways of my surroundings: "So do not act like the people in Egypt, where you used to live, or like the people of Canaan, where I am taking you. You must not imitate their way of life" (Leviticus 18:3 NLT).

We have to be careful—many things that are lawful are not expedient for believers. In my next book, I will expose the lawful activities and feasts that are driving believers away from the heart and affection of God without their recognizing it because of the subtle nature of the enemy's ways. God told the children of Israel not to learn the ways of the people in lands or places He would bring them to.

Let's look at the ecclesiastical side. This is a crucial area especially for new or young believers. Babies are born with no habits, no sense of right or wrong, and no knowledge of the world. They learn from their environments and those who take care of them. Whatever they learn will become their norms, morals, and beliefs, and they will look at the world through those lenses. Just as newborns do, new converts will go through a similar process. In essence, pastors become their spiritual parents; they will shape and mold the new converts' spiritual lives. Believers must know the scriptures: "Study to shew thyself approved unto God, a workman that needeth not to be ashamed, rightly dividing the word of truth" (2 Timothy 2:15). It is the believers' responsibility to develop themselves spiritually.

> Dear friends, you always followed my instructions when I was with you. And now that I am away, it is even more important. Work hard to show the results of your salvation, obeying God with deep reverence and fear. (Philippians 2:12 NLT)

Unfortunately, false teachers have entered the world. Jesus told His disciples about the signs of the last days: "Take heed that no man deceive you" (Matthew 24:4). Believers who don't know the scriptures will be easy prey for Satan's tactics and in danger of falling away from God. Jude 1:4 (NLT) reads,

> I say this because some ungodly people have wormed their way into your churches, saying that God's marvelous grace allows us to live immoral lives. The condemnation of such people was recorded long ago, for they have denied our only Master and Lord, Jesus Christ.

The apostle John wrote about what was happening in the church God was sending warnings to through His servant.

> But I have a few complaints against you. You tolerate some among you whose teaching is like that of Balaam, who showed Balak how to trip up the people of Israel. He taught them to sin by eating food offered to idols and by committing sexual sins. (Revelation 2:14–15 NLT)

Scripture warns us,

> For a time is coming when people will no longer listen to sound and wholesome teaching. They will follow their own desires and will look for teachers who will tell them whatever their itching ears want to hear. They will reject the truth and chase after myths. (2 Timothy 4:3–4)

I want to provide a scripture in two different versions; listen to God's Word.

> Some people may contradict our teaching, but these are the wholesome teachings of the Lord Jesus Christ. These teachings promote a godly life. Anyone who teaches something different is arrogant and lacks understanding. Such a person has an unhealthy desire to quibble over the meaning of words. This stirs up arguments ending in jealousy, division, slander, and evil suspicions. These people always cause trouble. Their minds are corrupt, and they have turned their backs on the truth. To them, a show of godliness is just a way to become wealthy. (1 Timothy 6:3–5 NLT)

And now the other version.

> If any man teach otherwise, and consent not to wholesome words, even the words of our Lord Jesus Christ, and to the doctrine which is according to

> godliness; He is proud, knowing nothing, but doting about questions and strifes of words, whereof cometh envy, strife, railings, evil surmisings, Perverse disputings of men of corrupt minds, and destitute of the truth, supposing that gain is godliness: from such withdraw thyself. (1 Timothy 6:3–5 KJV)

All Christian believers should carefully evaluate the beliefs and practices of a church by the standards of God's Word and associate with and support a church that meets the New Testament standards (Matthew 18:17; Acts 2:42; Matthew 28:19).

Please remember that not everyone in the church is there for the same purpose; I found that out the hard way. In my spiritual youth, I learned the ways of my environment and slightly fell away from the truth because I was doing what I saw. That ended very quickly. Many of my hurts, disappointments, and errors in teaching came from the church; I really had to understand what it meant for one to "study to shew thyself approved unto God, a workman that needeth not to be ashamed, rightly dividing the word of truth" (2 Timothy 2:15).

It was at that time that I started my quest to learn about my heavenly Father, and I began recognizing many errors, misquoted scriptures, and spiritual manipulations used by the men and women in churches. I did not want to learn in parts; I wanted a clear picture of the beginning to the end. That way, I could help others who were passionate about the truth as I was and those new babes in church. I wanted to make sure their spiritual lives were built on truth.

I wrote about my experience at the lake and my constraint—the lifejacket—that kept me from the depths I wanted to explore. Now, however, I can go to the depths of spiritual matters: "Deep calls to deep in the roar of Your waterfalls; all Your breakers and Your billows have swept over me" (Psalm 42:7 Holmes Christian Standard Bible). And referring to my tree-climbing days, I am not afraid of descending because now I realize that to go to the heights, I had to go to the depths first. I believe this is why I started swimming before climbing; before I go up, I must go down.

The focus is on the idea. Maybe by now, it is obvious where all this is heading. Here is a key point.

> Do not be unequally yoked with unbelievers. For what partnership has righteousness with lawlessness? Or what fellowship has light with darkness? What accord has Christ with Belial? Or what portion does a believer share with an unbeliever? What agreement has the temple of God with idols? For we are the temple of the living God; as God said, "I will make my dwelling among them and walk among them, and I will be their God, and they shall be my people. Therefore go out from their midst, and be separate from them, says the Lord, and touch no unclean thing; then I will welcome you." (2 Corinthians 6:14–17 ESV)

I'm not saying I am too holy to be around sinners; what I am saying is that we are to be the light of the world that cannot be hidden. We are to be the salt of the earth that does not lose it savor. Jesus ate with sinners, sat with tax collectors, and broke racial barriers. Jesus came not for those who were well but for those who were sick and needed a physician; He touched the blind, the deaf, and the lame, and He raised the dead. He cast out demons and faced Satan down. He had doubters, haters, and deniers following Him, and He had betrayers who wanted Him crucified. We must be around sinners to draw them to God.

Here is what I am getting to, the idea of what God wants: The life Jesus lived in public and His associates and friends in private is an uncompromised standard of holiness.

The idea is that our personal and spiritual lives should be so solidly grounded on Jesus's teaching that the gates of hell cannot prevail against it: "And I say also unto thee, That thou art Peter, and upon this rock I will build my church; and the gates of hell shall not prevail against it" (Matthew 16:18). Our personal and spiritual lifestyles should be compelling enough to draw others to Christ and to please God unconditionally. We are differently and uniquely remade when we are transformed; that is the idea. In the next chapter, this idea will generate an action plan.

CHAPTER 4

The Action Plan

> I beseech you therefore, brethren, by the mercies of God, that ye
> present your bodies a living sacrifice, holy, acceptable unto God,
> which is your reasonable service. And be not conformed to this world:
> but be ye transformed by the renewing of your mind, that ye may
> prove what is that good, and acceptable, and perfect, will of God.
> —Romans 12:1–2

Now that we put together the idea, the next step is to develop the action plan. Sounds fun, right? Hmmm. Remember my action plan for losing weight? Pick any new year that you resolved to lose X number of pounds. (I'll let you figure out what X meant to you then.) Right then, you were probably sincere in this declaration and commitment. However, did you count the cost? Did you create a plan? Or did you just start by waking up early or going after work to the gym to work out on every piece of equipment? If you did that, I'm pretty sure you woke up the next day very sore and threw in the towel. Don't feel bad; many have done the same thing the next day or perhaps the next week or month. The Bible addresses this issue: "For which of you, intending to build a tower, sitteth not down first, and counteth the cost, whether he have sufficient to finish it?" (Luke 14:28).

Earlier, I gave you what could be an action plan for losing weight. Let's begin what a suitable action plan would look like to achieve a transformed life. To build the right action plan, you have to come up with accurate details to complement the idea, and keep in mind that the idea has two parts: personal and ecclesiastical.

I beseech you therefore, brethren, by the mercies of God, that ye present your bodies a living sacrifice, holy, acceptable unto God, which is your reasonable service. And be not conformed to this world: but be ye transformed by the renewing of your mind, that ye may prove what is that good, and acceptable, and perfect, will of God. (Romans 12:1–2)

That passage presents an action plan.

1. Present my body
2. Become a living sacrifice
3. Be holy and acceptable
4. Be not conformed to this world
5. Be transformed
6. Renew my mind
7. Prove what is good
8. Prove what is acceptable
9. Prove what is perfect
10. Know the will of God

These ten areas are what we need to do to transform our lives from our former images to our new images; 1 Thessalonians 4:4 (NLT) states, "Then each of you will control his own body and live in holiness and honor." The first part of the action plan is to learn how to possess, control, and discipline oneself at all times. In doing that, numbers 1 through 3 will be satisfied.

Self-control and discipline are challenging actions for some especially depending on their ages. You have to bring your body into alignment with the holy scriptures. You are the sacrifice. You must keep yourself from becoming spotted, blemished, or wrinkled by worldly activities. You cannot allow temptations to cause you to sin against number 3, being holy and acceptable.

Number 4 says, "Be not conformed to this world" Again, the Greek word conformed is *syschematizo*, meaning to conform one's self to another's pattern or to the popular worldview that rejects God and His revelation. These are things you cannot pattern yourself after.

> When you follow the desires of your sinful nature, the results are very clear: sexual immorality, impurity, lustful pleasures, idolatry, sorcery, hostility, quarreling, jealousy, outbursts of anger, selfish ambition, dissension, division, envy, drunkenness, wild parties, and other sins like these. Let me tell you again, as I have before, that anyone living that sort of life will not inherit the Kingdom of God. (Galatians 5:19–21 NLT)

> Those who are dominated by the sinful nature think about sinful things, but those who are controlled by the Holy Spirit think about things that please the Spirit. So letting your sinful nature control your mind leads to death. But letting the Spirit control your mind leads to life and peace. For the sinful nature is always hostile to God. It never did obey God's laws, and it never will. That's why those who are still under the control of their sinful nature can never please God. (Romans 8:5–8 NLT)

You may feel overwhelmed at this point thinking how in the world you will keep your body, which you had exposed to those things above, from partaking in them any longer but keep it in line. This is only the action plan. If your mind is constantly in contact with those things through music, old relationships not severed yet, secret and illicit behaviors, or improper books, magazines, and movies, then yes, it will be overwhelming. Instead, think about "casting down imaginations, and every high thing that exalteth itself against the knowledge of God, and bringing into captivity every thought to the obedience of Christ" (2 Corinthians 10:5).

You do not have to allow your mind to be consumed with perverted thoughts, illegal actions, or supposedly good things such as too much television, Facebook, or other distractions. However, you do have to cast down all your evil thoughts that will cause you to sin by patterning yourself after this world, which is the second item on the action plan. Through disciplining yourself and casting down every evil imagination (covering numbers 1–4), you will be ready for number 5: be transformed. Nonetheless, before we look at transformed, we need to look at numbers 6–9, which deal with renewing your mind and proving what is good, acceptable, and perfect.

Looking at numbers 6–9, which ones cause you to be transformed? (Hint: you may have to go to the beginning of this chapter to reread the full scripture to have a clear understanding.) If you selected number 6, you picked correctly—by renewing your mind.

> But people who aren't spiritual <u>can't receive</u> these truths <u>from God's Spirit</u>. It all sounds foolish to them and they can't understand it, for <u>only those who are spiritual</u> can understand what the Spirit means. (1 Corinthians 2:14)

Any believers who have not experiencing the transformed life they're looking for should consider this step—repenting or changing their minds. Our thinking must be transformed from old, ungodly ways of thinking to new, godly ways of thinking—the third part of the action plan.

How can people change the way they think after repentance? Easy. Just as newborns have to learn from their environments, they have to surround themselves in God's Word.

> Speaking to yourselves in psalms and hymns and spiritual songs, singing and making melody in your heart to the Lord Giving thanks always for all things unto God and the Father in the name of our Lord Jesus Christ. (Ephesians 5:19–20)

> <u>Unto the pure all things are pure</u>: but <u>unto them that are defiled and unbelieving is nothing pure</u>; but even their mind and conscience is defiled.

> Also consider Titus 1:15: "Sanctify them through thy truth: thy word is truth." (John 17:17)

Study the holy scriptures, sing songs, make melodies in your heart, meditate day and night on God's Word, and give thanks to God for all the things He has done. Your mind will change and be in a position to fulfill numbers 7–9: to prove what is good, acceptable, and perfect. This is where it gets interesting—after your mind is changed and transformational thoughts are taking root, the heavy work begins through one strong word: *prove.*

As a new believer or mature believer, you have to test—prove—everything that is good, acceptable, and perfect. Remember, you are changing one form to another, so the behaviors you had before—the way you handled money, relationships, other people including foreigners, widows, and orphans, life activities, and customs—has to be tested to ensure they are acceptable to your new way of living. You, as the one desiring to be transformed, have to "*Trust* in the LORD with all thine heart; and lean not unto thine own understanding. In all thy ways *acknowledge* him, and he shall *direct* thy paths." When we prove what is good, acceptable, and perfect and when we trust God's way and acknowledge Him in all our ways, He will direct our paths and we will know His perfect will, which is the last part of the action plan.

Here is the action plan.

1. Discipline my body and align it to God's Word.
2. Cast down all evil imagination.
3. Change the way I think through repentance, studying God's Word, and songs/meditation.
4. Test or scrutinize everything to prove what is genuine.
5. Trust God.
6. Acknowledge God in all my ways.
7. Lean not on my own knowledge.
8. Look for God's way and direction even if it is contrary to my current ways and understanding.
9. Follow His ordered steps.

In this chapter, we examined in depth Romans 12:1–2 to understand the essentials of an action plan to support the idea we are searching for to transform into our new godly image. The next chapter will move us into the agreement.

CHAPTER 5
The Agreement

Can two walk together, **except they be agreed.**
—Amos 3:3

In first part of the book, I introduced a question to you: can two walk together? As discussed, the question prompts the idea and the idea draws the action plan, but unless these two are debated together, there cannot be an agreement. Notice in the later part of the scripture, it says, "except they be agreed." Who is the "they?" There must be at least two. And what is the agreement? We can see that at least two parties have to come together for a heart-to-heart dialogue about their common interests, and when both parties are satisfied with the terms of the agreement, they can write out and sign a contract and walk together, which speaks of a unity and submission to the other based on the contract. There is no longer room to go against the grain; there is no turning back or quitting because the contract was signed and it's time to begin.

Who are the two people walking together? If we are agreeing that there is unity and submission, who is the unity and submission to, and how will all this help us to walk it out? Before I answer that, let's pull all this together. Chapter 4 presented the idea (be transformed both personally and spiritually) and chapter 5 dealt with the action plan. I stated earlier that the idea prompts the action; the idea of losing weight leads to the action of doing so and committing to the plan. But from here, I will consider only the idea and agreement of a transformed life.

It's time to revisit that question: who are the two people walking together? The first is you. You were drawn into this contract the moment you realized this.

And you hath he quickened, <u>who were dead</u> *in trespasses and sins*; wherein in time past ye walked according to the course of this world, according to the prince of the power of the air, the spirit that now worketh in the children of disobedience: among whom also we all had our conversation in times past in the lusts of our flesh, fulfilling the desires of the flesh and of the mind; and were by nature the children of wrath, even as others.

But God, who is rich in mercy, for his great love wherewith he loved us, even when we were dead in sins, hath quickened us together with Christ, (by grace ye are saved;) and hath raised us up together, and made us sit together in heavenly places in Christ Jesus: that in the ages to come he might shew the exceeding riches of his grace in his kindness toward us through Christ Jesus. For by grace are ye saved through faith; and that not of yourselves: it is the gift of God: not of works, lest any man should boast. For we are his workmanship, created in Christ Jesus unto good works, which God hath before ordained that we should walk in them. (Ephesians 2:1–10)

When we realize we need a savior, we are the first person to enter the contract. We are willing to sit at the table to hear what God wants to say. We want our misery to go away, we want our pain to cease, we crave for pure love in all the right ways, we want our children in line, we want loving relationships with our spouses, children, and others, we want the right employment and wages, and we want everything in its proper order. Our brokenness caused our heart to hear and want a better way, a transformed way.

God moved on us when He saw our brokenness, and He saved us not by the righteous deeds we had done but according to His mercy, through the washing of new birth and renewal by the Holy Spirit (Titus 3:5). The two who are entering this agreement are you and the Holy Spirit.

Before Jesus departed His disciples, He told them, "And I will pray the Father, and he shall give you *another Comforter, that he may abide with you for ever*" (John 14:16). Jesus knows the hearts of His followers. Before He returned to the Father, He promised His followers another Comforter. Up to that point, Jesus had been their comfort, protection, provider, and more. The disciples saw firsthand the miracles, signs, and wonders that followed Jesus; they knew He was the Son of God.

Imagine how the disciples must have felt after living as devoted followers of Christ and sacrificing to be with Him day and night only to hear He was departing and they could not come where He was going. But Jesus promised to leave them a comforter. The Greek word for comforter is *paraklete*—one who comes alongside to help. Can two walk together? Can two be in submission to the other? Yes, if there is an agreement.

We who are now entering a new life with Christ have to submit our wills—our past ways of living and our futures, dreams, knowledge, and lives—to the Holy Spirit, who will empower us to fulfill the contract or agreement and walk with us. The Holy Spirit, our guide, brings back Jesus's words in John 16:13 to our memory. He speaks to us (Acts 13:2), He gives us strength (Judges 6:6, 15:14–15, 16:15–18), He make us bold (Acts 4:31), He teaches us (John 14:26), and so much more. Who better than the Holy Spirit could walk with us in our journey especially since we were assured He would never leave us even when times were tough? What a comfort to know we will never be alone in this walk. What a comfort to know we will have a guide and will not be on our own. What a comfort to know we will have a teacher who will make sure we understand what we need to do. In this walk, when we are weak and want to quit, He gives us strength. When we are afraid, He calms our fears and becomes our comfort; He empowers us to take courage to try.

> But as it is written, Eye hath not seen, nor ear heard, neither have entered into the heart of man, the things which God hath prepared for them that love him. But God hath revealed them unto us by his Spirit: for the Spirit searcheth all things, yea, the deep things of God. For what man knoweth the things of a man, save the spirit of man which is in him? even so the things of God

knoweth no man, but the Spirit of God. Now we have received, not the spirit of the world, but the spirit which is of God; that we might know the things that are freely given to us of God. Which things also we speak, not in the words which man's wisdom teacheth, but which the Holy Ghost teacheth; comparing spiritual things with spiritual. (1 Corinthians 2:9–13)

The Holy Spirit knows the way God has chosen for your life, and He knows how to get you there. He also knows your heart, your strengths and weakness, and your fears. He knows how to walk with you, and you must learn how to walk with Him through trust and submission through consistent prayer, fellowship, and communion. The Holy Spirit won't break the contract; He will be faithful through the whole process. He won't lie to you or abuse you. He is gentle, and He loves you. He is the best person to be in an agreement with. Are you ready for your journey to begin?

CHAPTER 6

Transformed: The Father's Image

For I know the thoughts that I think toward you, saith the LORD,
thoughts of peace, and not of evil, to give you an expected end.
—Jeremiah 29:11

Many are familiar with this scripture, but it became so real to me on March 9, 2012, the day my heart was crushed. I haven't shared much about my adult life. In 1993, seven years after serving in the military, I got married and had a daughter on my birthday. Fourteen months after her birth, I bore a son. My marriage was not ideal, which wounded my soul. After five long years, we divorced, but I did get the two best gifts ever from God.

Nonetheless, in 2012, just two months before she was to graduate from high school, my beautiful baby girl succumbed to diabetes at age eighteen. Believe it or not, I gave the eulogy, and the scripture the Lord echoed throughout the whole process was Jeremiah 29:11.

A concise version of the message was this: If I knew I had only eighteen years with my daughter, what would I have done differently? What would I have changed? What would I have planned? Where would I have taken her? What would I have exposed her to? The short time would have forced me to be very purposeful with her life. Her father and I had planned a life for her that included world travel (due to our military careers), successful completion of high school, graduating from college with a business degree, marriage, and children. All that seemed reasonable—the typical American Dream.

It was then that God began dealing with me because there was one thing I had failed to do as a parent—seek the plan He had for her life. I failed to align my thoughts with His. I failed to retrieve the blueprints and guide her through the course set for her life. When it came to an end, it was shorter than I had planned. There wasn't a high school or college graduation, there wasn't a marriage, and there weren't any children. I will never have mother-daughter luncheons or spa times with her, nor will I receive any more random text messages from her. My dearly beloved baby girl transitioned into a graduation I never considered; she and her brother were supposed to lay me to rest, not the other way around. Had I known God's plans for her, I would have been ready. Do you know the plans God has for you? Have you sought His blueprint of your life? Have you seen or discussed the contract?

"I am what God declares me to be" (Jeremiah 18:1–6). The word that came to Jeremiah from the Lord was,

> Arise, and go down to the potter's house, and there I will cause thee to hear my words. Then I went down to the potter's house, and, behold, he wrought a work on the wheels. And the vessel that he made of clay was marred in the hand of the potter: so he made it again another vessel, as seemed good to the potter to make it. Then the word of the LORD came to me, saying, O house of Israel, cannot I do with you as this potter? saith the LORD. Behold, as the clay is in the potter's hand, so are ye in mine hand, O house of Israel.

I shared with you a snapshot of my life. I was a marred vessel. Life got hold of me, and it wasn't pretty. How can God use a person like me? How can He turn something so damaged into something good? How can He transform me from filthy rags to righteousness?

In Jeremiah 18:1–6, God told Jeremiah to go down to the potter's house, where He would speak with him. Jeremiah got to the potter's house and saw the potter working at a wheel. But the vessel he made of clay was marred in his hand, so the potter made it again into another vessel shaping it as it seemed best to him. Then the Word of the Lord came to me "He said, O house of Israel, cannot I do with you as this potter?"

All my life comes down to this life-changing moment. This is where we submit to the Holy Spirit according to the Father's plans for us. We are to become images of him, that is, mental representations of Him. What God sees, He speaks, and what God speaks is created.

As I came across those in the Bible who were identified as having "walked with God," I remembered what Amos 3:3 asked: "Can two walk together?" "And Enoch walked with God: and he was not; for God took him." Noah walked with God in Genesis 6:9: "These are the generations of Noah: Noah was a just man and perfect in his generations, and Noah walked with God." These two walked with God after letting go of their ways.

We know little about Enoch, but we can examine Noah's life a bit more. Could Noah have created the ark in his own strength or power? The idea of the ark was outside the realm of his thinking. Genesis 2:5 reads, "And every plant of the field before it was in the earth, and every herb of the field before it grew: for the LORD God had not caused it to rain upon the earth, and there was not a man to till the ground." I imagine that after God explained His plan to Noah, he was overwhelmed by that because he could not conceive the idea or image, but he trusted God. After the two received everything, the agreement came into play and the action began. So what was the image? Noah's occupation went from being a husband, father, and farmer to being a carpenter and keeper of animals. He walked in the image of what God saw or selected for his life, and he became a yielded vessel to fulfill His plan.

Many other pillars from the Bible were like Noah. God gave Abram the blueprint for his life, and He gave his son, Isaac, and all future generations life. God visited Jacob (who became Israel) and changed the course of his life. Then it went from Joseph to Moses, to Joshua, to the prophets, to Jesus, and then to the apostles Simon to Peter, to Saul, to Paul, and now to you. All these led lives of their own until the timing of God was right and they were transformed.

The patriarchs in the Bible could have remained true to their personal desires and turned down God's call of God. But as the words of Mary, the virgin chosen by God, simply put it, "Behold the handmaid of the Lord; _be it unto me according to thy word_. And the angel departed from her" (Luke 1:38). The angel of God gave Mary the plan for her life. These servants of God humbled themselves to do His will and became all He saw them to be.

After living such a broken life, I was afraid of success. I experienced many people become vain because of their status, and I wanting no part of that lifestyle. In 2008, when I retired from the military and moved to a new area, the Lord promised me many things—a home, a job, and a car. I was quite satisfied with my paid-off vehicle, but the Lord told me to get the car of my dreams. My father loved restoring Mercedes-Benzes, and I developed the same love for those cars, which I considered luxurious.

Most would have run to get such a vehicle, but I dragged my feet. My heart was torn; I was afraid of becoming materialistic, but God assured me that would not happen. One day, my paid-off SUV, which had never caused me any problems, did not start. I had to laugh. I said, "God, you're playing with me, right?" and He said, "Out with the old and in with the new." God has a sense of humor. So I bought a Mercedes. There is, however, a balance to what I sought out. I had to come to grips with myself and realize that if God wanted something for my life, who was I to decide otherwise?

Another great event occurred when I was accepted into my doctoral program. Many Christians speak either positively or negatively about education. Some want the glory to be displayed through uneducated vessels like the disciples on the Day of Pentecost. Others esteem education as a high place with God as He is intellectual.

Midway through the program, I wanted to withdraw from it, but then I went to a movie with a friend, someone who had just completed a doctorate in education. I felt inferior as someone with only a master's degree who was considering leaving a doctoral program because I was unwilling to yield to expansion and deeper stretches needed to complete the program. I began sounding like Israel, which wanted only to walk in its own plans: "And they said, There is no hope: but we will walk after our own devices, and we will every one do the imagination of his evil heart" (Jeremiah 18:12). Had I not sat next to that person, I may have given in. I realized God had opened the door for me to be accepted into the program and would thus give me the ability to receive a doctorate. I girded myself to stay the course and complete the program. God's grace allowed me to will myself to submission and accept all He declared me to be!

The potter knows what's best for my life. Psalm 47:4 declares that He chose our inheritance for us. If I rebel against His choice, I can lose it all according to Jeremiah 18:7. We can choose our own way, but destruction is in our path, and God can reconsider the good He intended for us. We must submit to almighty God and become what He declares us to be. We will be like His Son, who never said a grumbling word. From this day forward, we should refuse to complain about whom God has chosen us to be. He has chosen us for destiny, and through His Holy Spirit, He will show us how to expand our lives to encompass it all.

Our capacity is unlimited because we are in Him and He is in us. Like Jeremiah, all we need is to see what we are to become and we will gracefully accept it. But even better, like Christ, He had a Word, God's Word. Jesus manifested every Word about Him written in the Law, the Psalms, and the prophets. Like Jesus, we will manifest whatever He speaks of us. If He wants me to earn a doctorate, I will. If He wants me to become a doctor, I will. If He wants me to become healed and whole, I will be. If He says I am to become an evangelizer, I will become an evangelizer. He says it, and I will become it—king, priest, kingdom builder; author, or pilot. I will become a submitted vessel.

We just discussed the physical aspect of transformation; let's discuss the spiritual.

The natural transformation is easy. Most people can accept challenges to be professionally successful, but to develop spiritually is more demanding because transformation will cause people to question every tradition, value, belief, and understanding they had been taught. If you're not ready to let all that go, you will struggle through the transformation process. Ready, set, transform!

Here is where it all begins. You must understand as a new believer or a more-focused believer that originally, God created humankind as perfect "So <u>God created</u> man <u>in his *own* image</u>, in <u>the image of God</u> created he him; male and female created he them" (Genesis 1:27). According to the Blue Letter Bible, the Greek word for "create" is *bara*, which means to shape, form, or fashion always with God as the subject.

We were originally made in the perfect image of God. Adam's heart, thoughts, and actions were pure, and he lived in an uncontaminated and faultless world. Until Adam disobeyed God's commandment, his world was perfect. Unfortunately, that lasted only about 130 years. A single choice changed humankind and the world until salvation came to redeem us and transform us back to the Father. But look at what happened next.

> Wherefore, as <u>by one man sin entered into the world</u>, and *death by sin*; and so <u>DEATH PASSED UPON ALL MEN</u>, for that all have sinned: (For until the law sin was in the world: but sin is not imputed when there is no law. Nevertheless <u>death reigned from Adam to Moses, *even over them that had not sinned*</u> after the similitude (equality; author's emphasis) *of Adam's transgression,* who is the figure of him that was to come. But not as the offence, so also is the free gift. For if through <u>the offence of one many be dead,</u> <u>much more the grace of God, and the gift by grace,</u> <u>which is by one man, Jesus Christ,</u> hath abounded unto many. And not as it was by one that sinned, so is the gift: <u>for the judgment was by one to condemnation,</u> <u>but the free gift is of many offences unto justification.</u> For if by one man's offence death reigned by one; much more they which receive abundance of grace and of the gift of righteousness shall reign in life by one, Jesus Christ.) Therefore as *<u>by the offence of one judgment came upon all men to condemnation</u>*; even so *<u>by the righteousness of one the free gift came upon all men unto justification of life.</u>* For as *<u>by one man's disobedience many were made sinners,</u>* so *<u>by the obedience of one shall many be made righteous</u>*. Moreover the law entered, that the offence might abound. But where sin abounded, grace did much more abound: That as <u>sin hath reigned unto death</u>, even so might <u>grace reign through righteousness unto eternal life by Jesus Christ our Lord.</u> (Romans 5:12–21)

Now let's examine this scripture: "And *Adam* lived an hundred and thirty years, and *begat a son in his own likeness, after his image*; and called his name Seth" (Genesis 5:3). Notice that Adam's son was in Adam's likeness; everything Adam became after the fall was passed down to his son, who was carrying the new DNA coding of sin. Everyone since has inherited Adam's sinful nature: "Behold, I was shapen in iniquity; and *in sin* did my mother conceive me" (Psalm 51:5). We started life as innocent as we could be dead in sin and needing a Savior.

So what needs transformation—the body or the heart? What happened to Adam in the garden? How many times did He die? Pay attention to these two scriptures.

> And *the Lord God commanded the man*, saying, Of every tree of the garden thou mayest freely eat: But of the tree of the knowledge of good and evil, thou shalt not eat of it: for *in the day* that *thou eatest* thereof *thou shalt* surely die.

Adam and Eve broke God's commandment by eating fruit from the Tree of the Knowledge of Good and Evil, which ended up putting us in our sinful state. But how many times did Adam die? The scripture tells us, "In THAT day that thou eatest thereof THOU SHALT SURELY DIE," If he would surely die when he ate the fruit at age 130, why did he live 800 more years? Ezekiel 18:20a says, "The soul that sinneth, it shall die." Adam was to live eternally in the garden, but because of his disobedience, God's judgment came upon him and his two deaths came about. Physically, Adam lost his eternal status and physically died 800 years after he sinned. Spiritually, Adam died as soon as he sinned. This is why God drove Adam and Eve from the garden; otherwise, all those who came after Adam in his image and likeness would have access to the Tree of Life and live eternally in sin.

> And the Lord God said, Behold, the man is become as one of us, to know good and evil: and now, lest he put forth his hand, and take also of the tree of life, and eat, and live for ever: therefore the Lord God sent him forth

from the garden of Eden, to till the ground from whence
he was taken. So he drove out the man; and he placed at
the east of the garden of Eden Cherubims, and a flaming
sword which turned every way, to keep the way of the
tree of life. (Genesis 3:22–24)

Now can you understand why spiritual transformation is a bit more
challenging than physical transformation? Nothing outside humanity
keeps us from external life—that includes the way we comb my hair, the
way we dress, where we work, or what we eat. "It's not what goes into
your body that defiles you; you are defiled by what comes from your
heart" (Mark 7:15 NLT).

Now we get to the good part! Mark wrote in his gospel, "You are
defiled by what comes from your heart." This is the root of what has to
be transformed! Our heart changes how we see things: "Unto the pure
all things are pure: but unto them that are defiled and unbelieving is
nothing pure; but even their mind and conscience is defiled" (Titus
1:15). Transformation is a heart matter. The prophet Jeremiah said it
best.

The heart is deceitful above all things, and desperately
wicked: who can know it? I the LORD search the heart,
I try the reins, even to give every man according to his
ways, and according to the fruit of his doings. (Jeremiah
17:9–10)

No one wants to admit his or her heart is deceitful above all things
or desperately wicked, but we cannot argue with the scriptures. God
knows our hearts; He searches our hearts and tries our hearts.

At one time, I examined where I stood in the eyes of the Lord to
see if my life conformed to His image. That, however, I could not do by
listing what I thought of my life good or bad but only through aligning
my life to God's Word. Only then could I clearly see the true image and
areas that still needed attention.

One day about ten years ago, God asked me through His Holy Spirit
if I would allow Him to teach me His way. I thought that before I could

do that, I would have to be willing to forget or let go everything I had learned, but because I loved God with all my heart even with some reservation of what that might mean, I said yes.

Being military, I traveled about every three years, and that meant relocating to different churches. I came to understand that many churches focused on traditional denominational teachings instead of on Jesus's and the apostles' teachings. I did not want part of denominational teachings because they were divisive: "Are you a Baptist? Or are you of the Holiness? Or are you of the Catholic faith? Perhaps the Church of God in Christ?" These divisions plague the church; that made my choice much easier.

You must be willing to lay it all down to truly be transformed. Are you ready and willing to take this next step? Here are two passages of scriptures that begin the process.

> When you enter the land the LORD your God is giving you, *be very careful not to imitate the detestable customs of the nations living there.* For example, never sacrifice your son or daughter as a burnt offering. And do not let your people practice fortune-telling, or use sorcery, or interpret omens, or engage in witchcraft, or cast spells, or function as mediums or psychics, or call forth the spirits of the dead. Anyone who does these things is detestable to the LORD. It is because the other nations have done these detestable things that the LORD your God will drive them out ahead of you. But you must be blameless before the LORD your God. The nations you are about to displace consult sorcerers and fortune-tellers, but the LORD your God forbids you to do such things. (Deuteronomy 18:9–14 NLT)

> Then the LORD said to Moses, "Give the following instructions to the people of Israel. *I am the LORD your God. So do not act like the people in Egypt, where you used to live, or like the people of Canaan, where I am taking you. You must not imitate their way of life.* You

must obey all my regulations and be careful to obey my decrees, for I am the LORD your God. If you obey my decrees and my regulations, you will find life through them. I am the LORD." (Leviticus 18:1–5 NLT)

God had chosen Israel to be a nation that lived in a way that reflected His image, nature, and characteristics to draw other nations to Him. Israel was not to take pleasure in other nations' false idolatries, religious practices, or sexual habits and more. Israel was to be obedient to God's call, but it was always being drawn to those who differed, and many times, God exiled or chastened the Israelites for that reason.

Can you relate to that? How often are you drawn from God because of others' habits and lifestyles especially when their practices seem lawful? Do you follow your ancestors' customs and traditions? Do you justify what you watch on television? Do you entertain gossip? Do you want only the kind of truth that keeps in line with how you want to live? This transformation is costly but liberating. Hear what God wanted for His people.

For you are a holy people to the LORD your God; the LORD your God has chosen you to be a people for His own possession out of all the peoples who are on the face of the earth. The LORD did not set His love on you nor choose you because you were more in number than any of the peoples, for you were the fewest of all peoples, but because the LORD loved you and kept the oath which He swore to your forefathers, the LORD brought you out by a mighty hand and redeemed you from the house of slavery, from the hand of Pharaoh king of Egypt. (Deuteronomy 7:6–8 NIV)

You have today declared the LORD to be your God, and that you would walk in His ways and keep His statutes, His commandments and His ordinances, and listen to His voice. The LORD has today declared you to be His people, a treasured possession, as He promised you, and

that you should keep all His commandments; and that
He will set you high above all nations which He has
made, for praise, fame, and honor; and that you shall be
a consecrated people to the LORD your God, as He has.
(Deuteronomy 26:17–19 NIV)

Sometimes, I wonder if people even like being different from others.
Do you want to walk as a foreigner in this world? Are you hungry for
God? Do you want to be set apart from this world? Do you wear this
world loosely, or are you skin-tight with its customs? Whose image are
you wearing? Are you trending with God or with the world? Will you be
like Lot's wife, who turned into a salt pillar when she was commanded
not to look back coming out of Sodom and Gomorra? Will you be the
sanctified? Will you be the justified? Can you endure the process? Will
you become the obedient and faithful bride of Christ?

The world is trying its best to undo what God has done by melting
away differences to unite people in an unholy way. In my next book, *The
Backward Mentality of Satan*, I will address in depth the unholy feast I
will introduce now.

To transform, let's revisit Romans 12:1–2.

I beseech you therefore, brethren, by the mercies
of God, that ye *present your bodies a living sacrifice,*
holy, acceptable unto God, which is your reasonable
service. And *be not conformed to this world*: but be ye
transformed by the renewing of your mind, that ye may
prove what is that good, and acceptable, and perfect,
will of God.

We have work to do here! Don't get me wrong; we are not trying to
earn salvation because that will never work. I am saying that according
to the scriptures, our reasonable service is to present our bodies as living
sacrifices. We are to maintain a holy and acceptable lifestyle; we are not
to look like or pattern ourselves after this world. We must renew our
minds so we can live in the good, acceptable, and perfect will of God.

He expects us to do this with the aid the Holy Spirit guiding us through this process.

Studying the Word of God will transform our minds and change us for the better. We know that when we know better, we do better. So when our mind is better, we are in a position to prove the good, acceptable, and perfect will of God.

This is the tricky part I believe we all get stuck at: we know a lot! Because of our knowledge whether due to formal education or life experiences, we bring that information into our new lives. If our knowledge itself was able to transform us, we would feel satisfied and justified by what we knew. Conversely, scriptures reveals this: "Trust in the LORD with all thine heart; and lean not unto thine own understanding. In all thy ways acknowledge him, and he shall direct thy paths" (Proverbs 3:5–6). Our knowledge is limited. We know what love is and feel no need to study it, right? This is one example of how commonly we error in judgment. God wants us to realize we cannot take for granted what we know. Love is simple to understand because everyone knows what it means, but if we really knew how to love, why is all this hatred and murder in the world? Why have we neglected widows, foreigners, and orphan? People will tell you that they know what love is, but do they know love according to God's way of knowing love? God is love! To know God is to know love, and all who don't know love don't know God and cannot know love. But that is the mind-set of those who want to be transformed from their image to God's image.

Every little thing we take for granted—how to love God and others, how to raise our children and treat our spouses, how to handle money, how to forgive, and so on—must be sought out for its truth through the Word of God and adopted into our lives; that must become habit. I have to prove traditions such as Christmas, Valentine's Day, April Fool's Day, Easter, and New Year's Day are right for me as a believer before I can say that these are not worldly feasts Satan has blinded the minds of God's people to draw their affection from Him. There are appointed feasts when humanity is to appear before God. Do you know what they are? Have you kept the prophetic timetable of the Lord? Do you know the origins of the names of the days of the week and the months? Do you lie to your children about the tooth fairy or Santa Claus coming down a chimney? Do you pass down traditions to your children without searching the scriptures for their authenticity?

To transform ourselves means putting ourselves in a neutral position with God and allow a shedding of old to accept the new. We should examine every aspect of our walks through God's Word. That will take effort, but the reward will be rich because we will be putting on God's image as we do.

> So I find this law at work: Although I want to do good, evil is right there with me. For in my inner being I delight in God's law; but I see another law at work in me, waging war against the law of my mind and making me a prisoner of the law of sin at work within me. What a wretched man I am! Who will rescue me from this body that is subject to death? Thanks be to God, who delivers me through Jesus Christ our Lord! So then, I myself in my mind am a slave to God's law, but in my sinful nature a slave to the law of sin. (Romans 7:21–25 NIV)

At one time, I paused to examine where I stood in the eyes of the Lord and if my life conformed to His image. That drew my attention to areas of my life that needed correction. I searched the scriptures for the roots of the issues that persisted in my life.

> For in my inner being I delight in God's law. (Romans 7:22 NIV)

> I love God's law with all my heart. (Romans 7:22 NLT)

Here is an area that will challenge believers. No one ever wants to admit his or her failures or inability to change. Most believers think they love God's Word and His law, but if this is true, why do we struggle in some areas and excel in others? I love God's Word and put many hours into reading and studying it, but I still come up short in certain areas. What allows me to be very aware of His ways but fall short at the same time?

> But *I see* another law working in me, waging war against
> the law of my mind *and* making me a prisoner of the law
> of sin at work within me. (Romans 7:23 NIV)

What other law is working in me? Why would it be waging war against the law of my mind? Why would this make me a prisoner of the law of sin working in me? What is the law dealing with riches or wealth? Why am I bound at the door and being held back?

My mind says one thing, but it sees something else. But this power in me has declared war against what I think will trap me into thinking something I don't want to do.

> Those *who live* according to the *flesh* have *their minds set
> on* what the *flesh desires*; but those *who live* in accordance
> with the *Spirit* have their *minds set on* what the *Spirit
> desires*. The mind *governed by* the flesh is death, but the
> mind *governed by* the *Spirit* is life and peace. The mind
> *governed by* the flesh is hostile to God; *it does not submit
> to God's law, nor can it do so.* Those *who are in the realm
> of the flesh cannot please God*. (Romans 8:5–8 NIV)

> This power makes me a slave to the sin that is still within
> me. (Romans 7:23b NLT)

The flesh wars against the Spirit and the Spirit against the flesh.

> Oh, what a miserable person I am! Who will free me
> from this life that is dominated by sin and death?

Paul realized the position he was in because of the power that worked against him from within made him a slave to what he could not get free from. He wondered who would free him of his dilemma, his prison.

Proverbs 3:9 states, "Honor the LORD with your wealth and with the best part of everything you produce." You should cheerfully give God the first or best 10 percent possible. Nevertheless, I guarantee that the moment you do, the war will rage against your mind by saying, "You are in lack! Why give? You will never get ahead in your bills by giving so much money away. The people in the church will misuse your money anyway, so you may as well do what you want with your money. God knows your heart; He will understand your use of your money for necessities." The words your flesh launches against you are meant to keep you from doing right by God. The flesh says, "Store up for yourself," but God says, "Be a cheerful giver." The flesh says, "Let others do for themselves," but God says, "Remember the foreigners, the poor, the widows, and the orphans." The flesh says, "Be selfish," but God says, "Be generous." You are in a war.

Do you feel like Paul did? Do you wonder how you will ever get free from what is imprisoning you? Do you want out? Faith is the key that unlocks that door, thank God! Jesus Christ, our Lord, is the answer, the master key to every lock. So you see how it is: in my mind, my heart, I want to obey God's Law and be a cheerful giver, but my sinful nature enslaves me to the pleasures of this world.

> *Do not* let sin control the way you live; *do not* give in to sinful desires. And *do not* go on presenting the members of your body to sin as instruments of unrighteousness; but *present yourself to God* <u>as those alive from the dead</u>, AND *your members as instruments of righteousness to God*. For <u>sin shall not be master over you</u>, for <u>you are not under law</u> but [you are] author's emphasis under grace. (Romans 6:12–14 NLT)

Sin is any violation of the divine law in thought or act. It also means to err, be mistaken, to wander from God's law. I veered away from it though I said I loved it. God's law creates boundaries for our lives. Loving God's Word shows respect for those boundaries, and those who love God will keep His commandments.

I can continue going forward in my way of thinking and treating money the same way I always have, and if I do, the same results and bad habits will continue to follow me.

> <u>Submit yourselves</u> therefore *to God*. <u>Resist the devil</u>, and <u>he will flee from you</u>. Draw nigh to God, and he will draw

nigh to <u>you</u>. Cleanse your hands, <u>ye</u> sinners; and purify <u>your</u> hearts, <u>ye</u> double minded. Be afflicted, and mourn, and weep: let <u>your</u> laughter be turned to mourning, and <u>your</u> joy to heaviness. Humble <u>yourselves</u> in the sight of the Lord, and he shall lift <u>you</u> up.

The more time we spend in the Word of God seeking what scriptures say about money or any other situation, the easier it will be for us to submit to God's way of being a good steward of our money. We will begin to trust God and know He will heal our money issues. We will know the law that once waged war against us will be cast out. We will be released from the prison of poverty or greed or whatever money issues have imprisoned us and be granted freedom. Money is only one area, though; other laws of the flesh work against us.

Now the works of the flesh are manifest, which are these; adultery, fornication, uncleanness, lasciviousness, idolatry, witchcraft, hatred, variance, emulations, wrath, strife, seditions, heresies, envyings, murders, drunkenness, revellings, and such like: of the which I tell you before, as I have also told you in time past, that they which do such things shall not inherit the kingdom of God. (Galatians 5:19–21)

The flesh loves these desires because the world considers them harmless. The world and the flesh expect everyone to accept everything. The wrong desires seem right and the right desires seem wrong. Nonetheless, these fleshly desires war against the Spirit.

This is the challenge of living a transformed life. This is the resistance the believer must overcome to escape the prison of death (although the believer is freed by the blood of Jesus) to live a transformed life. Here is our hope to live the transformed life.

Behold, the days come, saith the LORD, that <u>I will make a new covenant</u> with the house of Israel, and with the house of Judah: not according to the covenant that I made with their fathers in the day that I took them by the hand to bring them out of the land of Egypt; which my covenant they brake, although I was an husband unto them, saith the LORD: but this shall be the covenant that I will make with the house of Israel; After those days, saith the LORD, I will put my law in their inward parts, and write it in their hearts; and will be their God, and they shall be my people. And they shall teach no more every man his neighbour, and every man his brother, saying, Know the LORD: for they shall all know me, from the least of them unto the greatest of them, saith the LORD: for I will forgive their iniquity, and I will remember their sin no more. (Jeremiah 31:31–34)

God put His presence in you to bring you to life.

The Spirit of God, who raised Jesus from the dead, lives in you. And just as God raised Christ Jesus from the dead, he will give life to your mortal bodies by this same Spirit living within you. (Romans 8:11 NLT)

You cannot transform yourself, but if you submit to the Holy Spirit, He will transform your life.

But Jesus beheld *them*, and said unto them, With men this is impossible; but with God all things are possible. (Matthew 19:26)

When you die, the transformed life begins, and His image and glory are reveled.

If then you have been raised with Christ, seek the things that are above, where Christ is, seated at the right hand of God. Set your minds on things that are above, not on things that are on earth. For you have died, and your life is hidden with Christ in God. When Christ who is your life appears, then you also will appear with him in glory. (Colossians 3:1–4 ESV)

You must treat every area of your life no matter how great or small like the money scenario. If you are willing to walk away from all your former life and trust God, you will be able to resist the temptations of the devil, the lusts of the flesh will leave, your transformation will take place, and His image will appear. Just do not look back!

Concluding Reflections

I have seen sinners become new believers, and they crave developing like Christ. They are at every church service, every Bible study, every function and program every time the doors open (and on time, too—lol). New believers are hungry; they cry out to be closer to God and want the world to know about this new joy in their lives. Yet something happens and that zeal begins to fizzle out. Why is that? Most would say they had backslid or never had been serious about the commitment they made to God. Some old believers will say even worse things about them.

I believe with all my heart that new believers were sincere when they came to the altar for salvation. They knew their lives were not right, and they sought to change that. Yet after a season of religion—doing only what they had observed older church members doing—they did only what they thought was expected of them such as choir rehearsal, youth ministry, usher board, armor bearer, and so on. Please do not get me wrong—those are good things to do—but the devil considers the best time to devour new converts is when they first come to salvation.

Who is giving the sincere milk of God's Word to the new babes? After a season, when the zeal wears off, what is left? Do the new babes still have the same passion to be Christlike? Have older saints gotten hold of them and convinced them that it does not take all that to be saved?

Here is the transformation: we are to leave Adam's image and return to God's image; we are to leave Adam's disobedience and obey Jesus. Those who are led by the Spirit are God's children. Fellowship in church with other believers is good, but it does not replace fellowship and time alone with the Holy Spirit.

If you are hungry and really want to transform from your image to His, examine your life right now. Are you trending with this world? Do you crave what the world says is success? Are you storing up treasures because of selfishness? When was the last time you cared for the sick, fed the hungry, or clothed the naked? Are you winking at and overlooking sin? Are you in gossip groups? Do you hate those who hate you? Are you fornicating? Are you a glutton? Do you laugh at evil done to others? Is your mouth closed when others say wrong things? Do you let people mock God? Are you highly independent? Do you struggle with pride or sexual sins? Do you rob God of offerings?

If you answered yes to any of these things, repentance is your first step in transforming. We know our wrongs. We have to invest time to ensure we are developing our souls with fear and trembling. We have to desire fellowship with the Holy Spirit. We have to be transformed from our image to His.

The life I was given became scarred. There was no way I could only check the Sunday morning service block to soothe my conscience. I needed more. I wanted more. I had deep scars, wounds, and pains. My soul cried out in anguish, but no one heard me. Everyone always thought I was so strong; I heard that repeatedly. My athletic abilities masked my shortcomings. My silence kept me from saying what I felt. I lived in agony and misery, but I never complained.

When I gave my life to Jesus, my void dissipated and I became purposed. The Holy Spirit took me by the hand and became my schoolmaster. He kept me from learning religion and led me through the Word to show me how to become an obedient child of God. I started following the example Jesus left us and learned the Father's ways and His righteousness. The Holy Spirt helped me see the errors of the Israelites, His chosen leaders, and those who walked away from Him, who rejected Him, and who used Him, and He showed me those who loved and esteemed Him.

The transformation is not instant; it is a process that takes time. God knows what we can handle; He promised not to put more on us than we could bear, but little by little, He causes us to face the sin and ugliness in our lives. God will make us look at Him and see our shortcomings and failures not so we can run from them but to bring them to Him with hopefulness, not shame, knowing He will restore our lives. He will put us on the potter's wheel and make another vessel out of us. He will transform our lives to His image if we let Him. He is waiting for us to agree with Him so we can walk together in agreement with the Holy Spirit.

The Father is transforming my life as a believer every day even as damaged as I was. Our heavenly Father is taking one area of my life at a time and showing me issues that cause me to remain in a broken state. The more I see my faults through His Holy Word, the more I see areas that I have not submitted to Him or in which I have not yet been transformed. He lovingly allows me to bring those areas to Him as He is the only one who can bring the necessary change to my soul. I have come a long way, but I still have a long way to go. But God! What was so out of balance is now leveling out. Only He can make beauty from ashes.

This is a lifelong process. Are you ready for it? Where are you struggling? First, pray and ask the Holy Spirit to identify the areas that still plague your life. Then, use the lines below to write out what he identifies. Try to do no more than three at a time. Spend quality time with each area in prayer. Learn to find the voice and leading of the Holy Spirit. The more consistent you are, the more He will manifest Himself to you. The Holy Spirit is real.

Holy Spirit, I ask you to show the reader, who have gotten to this point and may be in tears, their shortcomings. Holy Spirit, their hearts may be hurting, and they may feel cheated because few have taken time to teach them what Romans 12:1–2 really means when they confessed their need for a Savior and invited Jesus into their lives.

Holy Spirit, please hold the readers up until they willingly leave the old man behind and put on the new. Please, Holy Spirit, let them love you, the Father, and the Son with all their heart, mind, soul, and strength. Forgive their sins, cleanse their slate with your blood, and love them with your eternal love. Transform their soul into the image of the Father. In Jesus's name, amen!

I love you, and I will pray for you through this process.

1. _____
2. _____
3. _____

1. _____
2. _____
3. _____

Enjoy your fellowship through the scriptures. Do not rush it; if you are unsure of all the scripture that deals with the identified areas, google the scriptures that deal with a particular topic such as love, money, or relationships and you will find them. Read them and meditate on them; the Holy Spirit will guide you to what He wants you to know and learn, and then, you can apply the Word to your and others' lives.

Printed in the United States
By Bookmasters